The Laugh Challenge

Joke Book

Hugs and Kisses Edition

With Fun
Illustrations

Hundreds of Jokes
That Kids and Family
Will Enjoy

RIDDLELAND

Table of Contents

Getting mail on Valentine's Day is fun, and, despite all Valentine's Day cards having similar messages, each card has its unique style. Likewise, this book is divided into four individual chapters – cards, if you will; each of which has a unique form. Each card is special in its own way, and all are a pleasure to read. You can begin with any card you want.

Riddleland Bonus Book

http://pixelfy.me/riddlelandbonus

Thank you for buying this book. We would like to share a special bonus as a token of appreciation. It is a collection of 50 original jokes, riddles, and two super funny stories!

Join our **Facebook Group**
at **Riddleland for Kids** to get
daily jokes and riddles.

> "There is only one happiness in this life,
> to love and be loved." ~ **George Sand**

We would like to personally thank you for purchasing this book. *The Laugh Challenge Joke Book: Hugs and Kisses Edition* is different from other joke books. It is not meant to be read alone, but instead it is a game to be played with siblings, friends, family or between two people that would like to prove who is a better comedian. Time to see who has the funny bone in the family!

These jokes are written to be fun and easy to read. Children learn best when they are playing. Reading can help increase vocabulary and comprehension. Jokes also have many other benefits such as:

- **Bonding** – It is an excellent way for parents and their children to spend some quality time and create some fun and memorable memories.

- **Confidence Building** - When parents give the riddles, it creates a safe environment for children to burst out answers even if they are incorrect. This helps children to develop self-confidence to express themselves.

- **Improve Vocabulary** – Jokes are usually written in easy to advanced words, therefore children will need to understand these words before they can share the jokes.

- **Better reading comprehension** – Many children can read at a young age but may not understand the context of the sentences. Jokes can help develop the children's interest to comprehend the context before they can share the joke with their friends.

- **Sense of humor** – Funny creative jokes can help children develop their sense of humor while getting their brains working.

Card One
Question and Answer Jokes

"The most important thing in life is to learn how to give out love, and to let it come in." ~ **Morrie Schwartz**

This first card is full of questions. Valentine's Day is full of questions – Does she like me? Will he send me a card? Will mom give me chocolates? Why are there pictures of a toddler in diapers shooting arrows? And who was this Valentine dude people talk about? So, it is fitting this book begins with questions as well. Questions lead to answers, and answers lead to wisdom – or, in the case of jokes, a smile.

Whether you are reading the jokes to yourself to get you in the Valentine spirit, sharing the joke with a friend, or even reading the question and letting your friend read the answer, these jokes are sure to entertain.

Why did the corn fall in love with the crow?

It whispered sweet nothings in its ear.

Why did the lady not marry the gardener?

He was too rough around the hedges.

What did the astronaut tell his girlfriend?

"You make me feel out of this world."

Why are some people so relaxed on Valentine's Day?

They take the time to stop and smell the roses.

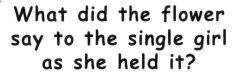

Why did the girl break up with the magician?

He disappeared before the wedding.

What did the flower say to the single girl as she held it?

"Are you looking for some buddy to love?"

Why did the phone and the smart watch break up?

There was no connection.

What did the girl gasp when the floral delivery agent brought her an unexpected bouquet on Valentine's Day?

"What in carnation?"

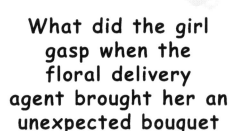

Why did the chocolate go to the dentist?

To get a new filling.

What happened when the candle found its match on Valentine's Day?

It lit up.

Was the popular girl impressed with the flower the poor boy had saved his money to give her?

No. She thought it was just one of rose things.

What do teenage girls often ask each other on Valentine's Day?

Are you feeling bouquet?

Do you think the tailor can repair his romantic relationship?

He's hanging on by a thread.

How is true love like a man's beard?

It never ends; it only grows.

What are you doing if you describe Valentine chocolates?

Making candied observations.

When the skydivers had an opportunity to go skydiving hand-in-hand on Valentine's Day, what did they do?

They jumped at it.

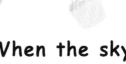

How did the onion propose to his girlfriend?

With a ring.

Cupid is sometimes called Stupid Cupid because of the odd combinations of people he brings together; what is he called when he makes ice-cream cones?

Scoop-it Cupid.

Why did the snake fall in love with her trainer?

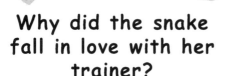

He was a real charmer.

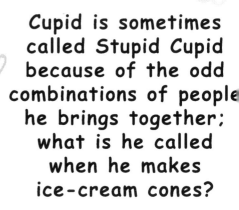

Why did the man keep loving his wife even though she made him switch from butter to margarine and she insisted on reading poems she had written?

At the wedding he said he would take her for butter or for verse.

What did one bowling pin say to another?

"Let's never split."

What did the kangaroo say to his girlfriend?

"Hop! in the name of love."

What do you call a boyfriend on Twitter who lives miles away?

Your tweet-heart.

Did bow-shooting Cupid think the boy and girl standing by the water fountain were a good match?

He thought they were worth a shot.

What happened when the flower stained the man's shirt and the man got angry?

His girlfriend noticed the man had a violet streak she had never seen before.

What happened when the Valentine's Day flower got embarrassed watching the boy and girl kiss?

The flower turned a little rosier.

How do young Valentine flowers greet each other?

"Hey, bud."

How do teenage Valentine flowers greet each other?

"How's it growing?"

How fast does Cupid make his wooden arrows?

A whittle at a time.

What happens when you're in love with a librarian?

Instead of the librarian checking your books out, you check out the librarian.

What do you call it when Cupid accidently hits two men with one arrow, making them fall for the same woman?

That's two in a row [arrow].

Do you feel sorry for the orchestra members that have to work on Valentine's evening playing romantic music?

They are there by choice; I have no symphony for them.

How can you tell if the cheapskate who eats in the dark to save electricity is being romantic or just frugal when you go to his house for a candlelight dinner?

If he actually lights the candle, he's being romantic.

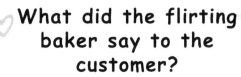

What did the flirting baker say to the customer?

"I only have pies for you."

Where did the two carrots go on their first date?

To the salad bar.

What kind of argument did the couple have regarding the storage building?

A he shed/she shed argument.

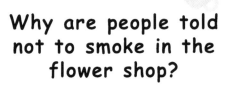

Why are people told not to smoke in the flower shop?

To prevent florist fires.

What kind of flower should never be placed in a vase?

Cauliflower.

What did the duck say to his girlfriend?

"I will quack up if you won't be my Valentine.'

Why did the boy give his girlfriend a dictionary?

It was a gift full of meaning.

How does the florist drive on Valentine's Day?

She puts the petal to the metal.

What is Cupid's favorite take-out food?

Wings; Cupid is often pictured with wings.

Why did always-hungry bow-shooting Cupid sign up for archery at camp?

He thought the counselors said, "Who wants a cherry?" instead of "Who wants archery?"

How did the girl find the warlock to be?

Charming.

What card game is popular on Valentine's Day?

Hearts.

What did the tomboy say about having red ribbons in her hair on Valentine's Day?

"I don't wear bows; I shoot them."

When Cupid is applauded, what does he like to do?

Take a bow. And an arrow.

What did the chef say to his Valentine?

"You look delicious."

What did the marshmallow say to the hot chocolate?

"I melt when I'm around you."

What happened when the teenage girl dated the magician?

It was magic.

What did the volcano say to his Valentine?

"I lava you."

What did the glue tell his girlfriend?

"I'm stuck on you."

17

Is it easy being Cupid?

No. It's heart work.

What did the male knife say to the female knife when he saw how she was dressed?

"Looking sharp!"

What did the nerd say to his Valentine?

"You're as sweet as pi."

What did the fast-food employee say to his Valentine?

"I only have fries for you."

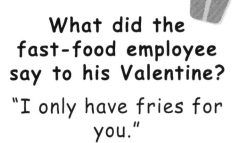

How are Wi-fi and a prospective Valentine alike?

You need to make a connection to be able to continue.

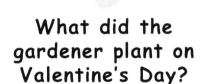

What did the gardener plant on Valentine's Day?

Kisses.

What happened when the boy first saw the new girl next door on that November morning when temperatures were below freezing?

It was love at frost sight.

What do guy ghosts say to girl ghosts?

"Hello, boo-tiful."

What did the card-dealing fortune teller tell her Valentine?

"It's in the cards."

What did the bowling ball say to the bowling pin on Valentine's Day?

"You're right up my alley."

What flowers do ghosts give to their ghoulfriends?

Moaning Glories and Merry Ghouls.

What did the sharp dresser say to the other sharp dresser on Valentine's Day?

"We're perfectly suited for each other."

What do you call it when the bachelor barely misses getting hit by Cupid's arrow?

An arrow escape.

What's it called when Cupid dresses like a thug and shows off his muscles?

Tough love.

How did the leatherworker feel about getting to make Cupid's arrow holder?

He quivered with delight.

What did the male astronaut say to the female astronaut as they blasted through space in their rocket on Valentine's Day?

"There may not be any gravity, but I'm still falling for you."

What do you call the Valentine's Day meal?

A hearty dinner.

How do you develop an interest in flowers?

Plant a few seeds and they will grow on you.

What did the Krispy Kreame Donut Factory employee tell his girlfriend?

"Donut go breaking my heart."

What did the welder say to his girlfriend on Valentine's Day?

"The sparks are certainly flying, aren't they?"

What makes the flowers a ghost gives his ghoul-fiend so special?

Ghosts put the "boo" in bouquet.

Cupid has wings, but sometimes he likes to ride; what does Cupid travel in?

An arrow-plane.

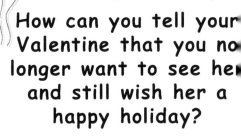

What did the flirt say to the nurse?

"You've got to help me. Cupid just shot me through the heart."

How can you tell your Valentine that you no longer want to see her and still wish her a happy holiday?

"Happy Independence Day."

What did one lollipop coo to the other lollipop on Valentine's Day?

"I'm a sucker for you."

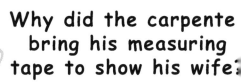

Why did the carpenter bring his measuring tape to show his wife?

He wanted to prove his love for her was beyond measure.

What did the barista tell her Valentine?

"You're my cup of tea."

What did the caveboy say to the cavegirl on Valentine's day?

"Want to make some history?"

What did the florist answer when asked how his business was?

He said his business was blooming.

What did the thesaurus say to the dictionary?

"You add meaning to my life."

Which is the most romantic vegetable?

The artichoke is all heart.

What did the photographer say to his Valentine?

"I can picture us together."

What are the wedding photographer's favorite flowers?

Posies.

How did the snake seal the card to his girlfriend?

With a hiss.

Is Cupid capable of convincing someone to fall in love?

His argument – at least his arrow – is very pointed.

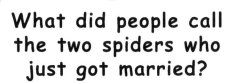

What did people call the two spiders who just got married?

Newly webs.

What happened when the musician's girlfriend saw him looking at other women?

He got in treble.

24

Why did the skeleton mistreat his date?

He had no heart.

What did the musician give his girlfriend on Valentine's Day?

A love note.

What did the doe tell the buck on Valentine's Day?

"I'm fawning for you."

25

What did the man who had pet rabbits say to his Valentine?

"No bunny compares to you."

What did the beaver say when his jealous wife accused him of looking at other females?

"There is no otter; just you."

Why did the girl make her boyfriend waffles?

Because she loved him a waffle lot.

Why was the numeral one standing in a cantaloupe?

He wanted to be somebody's one in a melon.

What kind of conversation do flirty, young women seek?

Engaging.

What did the baker say to his sweetheart?

"I racked my grain all night long, and I never thought of anyone prettier than you."

When is wedding cake like a golf ball?

When it's been sliced.

What did Dad say when Mom asked him to call her later?

"Hey, Later, you're kind of cute!"

What did the coloring book say to the crayons on Valentine's Day?	What did the romantic magician say before he disappeared?
"You color my world."	"Ho-kiss, Po-kiss."

What did the cheese say to the hamburger patty on Valentine's Day?

"I melt in your presence."

Why did the girl give her Valentine bananas?

Because she loved him bunches.

What did the stew say to the spoon?

"Peas be my Valentine."

What sweets did the skeleton give to his girlfriend for Valentine's Day?

Bone-bones.

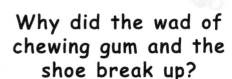

What did the pig farmer give his wife on Valentine's Day?

Hogs and kisses.

Why did the wad of chewing gum and the shoe break up?

The shoe thought the gum was a bit too clingy.

What did the flirting girl say to the janitor?

"You sweep me off my feet."

What do you call a boy and girl who date while in cooking school?

Taste buds.

Did you hear about the two little fish that fell in love?

It was guppy love.

What did the rabbit coo to his Valentine?

"There is no bunny like you!"

What happened when the self-centered guy kissed his one true love?

He left lip-prints on the mirror.

What happened when the girl met the zombie?

It was love at first fright.

What can you say in self-defense when your mom asks you if you are taking your brother's Valentine's candy?

"Not really. I'm just helping him share."

What did the man say to the witch when he fell in love with her?

"You've got me under your spell."

Where are dating apps pre-installed on computers?

On the heart drives.

Why did the zombie want to date the smartest girl in class?

Zombies love girls with brains.

How could Cupid improve his aim?

With better arrow dynamics.

What food changes a woman from a flirt to a loyal mate?

Wedding cake.

Why did the boy put cologne on his axe before picking up his date?

He wanted to speak with a slight axe scent.

What word did the unmarried girl think sounded the best in the whole world?

She thought "marriage" had a nice ring to it.

The teacher had her students make Valentine's Day cards and then she graded them. What grade did she assign?

Be Mine/us.

What's a good chat up line for you to use if you want to flirt with Frankenstein's monster?

"You are quite well put together."

Is bow-shooting Cupid skilled at matchmaking people into relationships?

He's been known to pull some strings - bow strings.

What did the flirting girl say to the locksmith?

"You hold the key to my heart."

What did the trout say to his girlfriend?

"Although there are other fish in the sea, you're the greatest catch!"

What do you call ants who go for meandering moonlit walks?

Roam ants.

Why did the newlyweds plant an apple tree?

They wanted to live apple-ly ever after.

Besides the class heartthrob, what else has thirteen hearts?

A deck of playing cards.

What did the bacon say to the tomato on Valentine's Day?

"Lettuce get together."

How did Cupid get an arrow stuck in his forehead after listening to the motivational speaker?

The speaker said to aim for the skies; Cupid did, but the arrow came back down and hit him.

How is blood like love?

It comes from the heart.

What's one nice thing about online dating apps?

You must click with each person.

Why was the girl so upset when her boyfriend took her to the gym on Valetine's Day?

Because the boxing ring was not the kind of ring she wanted to see.

What did the corn cob say to the other corn cob?

"I know this may come across as corny, but would you be my Valentine?"

What did the lightbulb whisper to his girlfriend?

"I love you a watt."

What did the Coke say to the Pepsi?

"I soda like you."

What did the male turkey coo to the female turkey?

"I can't help fowling in love with you."

Why should you keep your preferred choice of vowel a secret?

If you walk around saying, "I love u," people begin to think romantic thoughts.

Where did the bull and the cow go for their Valentine's date?

The moo-vies.

What did the sculpture proudly say to his girlfriend?

"I love you with all my art."

What did the ice cream coo to the butterscotch syrup?

"You're kind of sweet."

Why did the two students in the course America 1600- 1865 fall in love?

They had history together.

What did the tree call to the lumberjack on Valentine's Day?

"I'm falling for you."

What did the male dolphin tell the other female dolphin on Valentine's Day?

"You're my porpoise for living."

What did the cheese tell the cracker when they broke up?

I'm sorry. I'm just so much more mature than you are."

How did the dentist and the manicurist do on their date?

They fought tooth and nail.

Why did the Eskimo decide not to get married at the last minute?

He got cold feet.

What did one candle coo to the other candle on Valentine's Day?

"You light up my life."

How do baby chickens that are in love dance?

Chick to chick.

What kind of flowers cast a romantic glow?

Light bulbs.

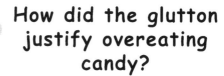

What did one oar suggest to the other oar on Valentine's Day?

"Do you want to put the "row" in romance?

How did the glutton justify overeating candy?

"Cupid missed the girl but hit the candy."

Sugar and cream were both happy being single; what happened when they got married?

It was the icing on the cake.

What kind of date did the two dancers have?

A tappy one.

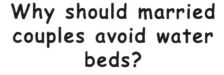

Why should married couples avoid water beds?

They might drift apart.

What did the Pilates instructor say as she relaxed with her boyfriend?

"Without you, my life is pure squat."

Who is the most popular high school teacher on Valentine's Day?

The history teacher has known lots of dates.

Why couldn't the macho man become a heart surgeon?

He only knew how to break hearts.

What kind of an evening did the pasta have with the hot water?

Strained.

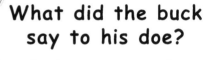

What is the bride and groom's favorite ride at the amusement park?

The marry-go-round.

What did the buck say to his doe?

Let's have some fawn.

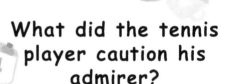

What kind of flowers should you buy your loved one if you made a mistake and need forgiving?

Oopsie Daisies.

What did the tennis player caution his admirer?

"Love means nothing to me."

What was the bee searching for on Valentine's Day?

His honey.

What happened when the boy fell in love with the girl next door?

They had a lawn-distance relationship.

What warning label should come on all chocolate?

Warning: Eating chocolate may cause your clothes to shrink.

Why did the flirty waitress ask the customer to read what it said on the menu?

It read "Me-n-u."

Why did the boy give his girlfriend grapes for Valentine's Day?

He wanted to show he loved her more than a bunch.

Why did the baseball urler and the softball hurler get married?

They were the pitcher perfect couple.

Who gets the most Valentine's Day cards?

The postal carrier (but they aren't all his to keep).

Card Two
Puns

"A spark of kindness starts a fire of love."
~ **Unknown**

A pun is a play on words. Many words have multiple meanings and in other cases the sound that makes one word also makes a word with a different meaning, such as "bear" and "bare". When one hears a word, one's mind goes down a track, in a pun, one suddenly realizes that one could have chosen the other track as well.

Puns are notorious for producing smiles – and who does not want to see a loved one smile. Share these jokes and put a smile on their face – and your face.

Did you hear about the accent Cupid's bow has?

It speaks with a twang.

What did the sheep say to his girlfriend?

"I love ewe, and I always wool."

What piece of wood is highly sought on Valentine's Day?

A match.

Why was the girl more impressed with the e-card than with her initials being carved into a tree?

She preferred something with more byte and less bark.

Why was the comedian's bride worried about her wedding reception?

She worried it was a terrible joke because all she could see was a long punch line.

What did the doe say to the buck on Valentine's Day?

"You're such a deer."

At the rehearsal dinner, what did Dad say when asked if he would say a word?

"A word."

What is the most popular paper product in the house on Valentine's Day?

The calendar; it has the most dates.

What are the best Valentine gifts made from?

Wooed.

What did the steaming bowl of chili say to the beautiful Saltine cracker on Valentine's Day?

"I'm not the only thing that's hot around here."

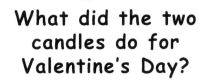

What did the two candles do for Valentine's Day?

They went out together.

What did the boy zombie say to the girl zombie on Valentine's Day?

"Do you believe in a dead romance?"

42

How did the boy and girl ball-point pens do on their date?

They clicked.

What did the cook say to her Valentine, the chef?

"You whisked me off my feet."

What happened when the cook fell in love with the chef?

He desserted her.

What did the male tightrope walker say to the female tightrope walker?

"Do you want to try online dating?"

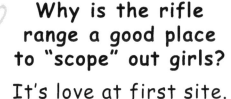

Why is the rifle range a good place to "scope" out girls?

It's love at first site.

What did the refrigerator say to the freezer on Valentine's Day?

"You're the coolest one I know."

Why was the girl tidepool so impressed with the boy tidepool?

He had big mussels.

Why didn't the archeologist get along well with his girlfriend?

He kept digging up her past.

Why did Dad stop by the local bakery on his way home from work on Valentine's Day?

To get Mom some flours.

How did the tailor's date with the seamstress go?

So-so.

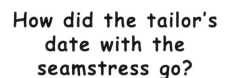

What happened to the romance between the red blood cells?

It was all in vein.

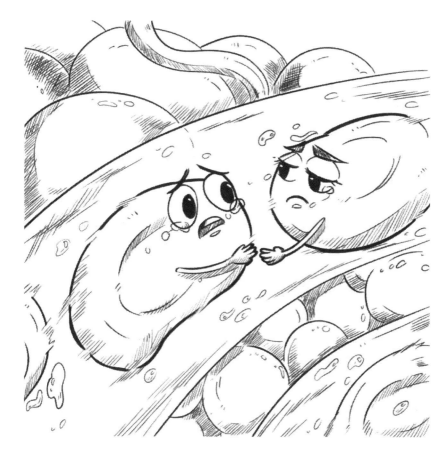

How do you describe Cupid when he uses his feet to draw back the bow to shoot the arrow?

Bow-legged.

Why did the boy think he was in love with the girl who worked at the pet shop?

She gave him butterflies.

Can arrows fall in love?

Many spend time with their bow.

What do trees have that most girls want?

Rings.

Why was the Valentine candle tired?

There's no rest for the wicked.

Was the candle happy the romantic Valentine's Day dinner was over?

It was delighted.

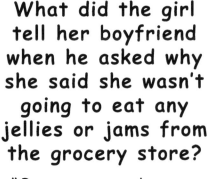

What did the girl tell her boyfriend when he asked why she said she wasn't going to eat any jellies or jams from the grocery store?

"Because you're my jam!"

Why was the girl disappointed when the boy put his and her initials in the tree trunk?

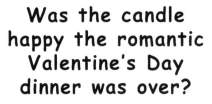 He wasn't willing to go out on a limb for her.

What happened when the two candles started dating?

They went out.

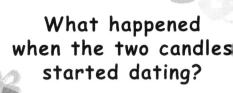

Why did the boy tear a Valentine in half and only give one piece to his so-called girlfriend?

It was a half-hearted effort.

What did Dad call the coffee beans as he prepared the rehearsal dinner?

Grounds for celebration.

How did the computer whiz ask a girl for a date?

"Do you want to grab a byte?"

What bean got jealous when his girlfriend talked to the corn?

The green bean.

Why did the astronomer refer to his female Valentine as "son"?

Because she was the center of his universe.

How did the couple do on their camping trip?

They had in tents feelings.

Why did the girl go out with the mushroom?

Because he's a fungi to be with.

Why did the girl agree to go on a date with the exterminator?

He promised he would quit bugging her if she did.

Their date was going great, but what happened when the boy swatted the bee that was flying around his girlfriend' face?

It was a buzzkill.

What kind of date did the two teachers have?

A classy one.

How did the ghost flirt with the jack o' lantern?

"Your smile lights up the room."

How did the author praise his girlfriend on Valentine's Day?

By saying, "You're all write."

What did the computer say to the keyboard on Valentine's Day?

"You are my type."

What did the racecar driver say to his Valentine?"

"Not only do you make my heart race, I know I'm on the right track."

What did the black widow spider say to her new boyfriend?

"I met my first husband on the web."

What kind of deal did Cupid find when he shopped for a second-hand bow?

One with no strings attached.

What did one tree branch say to its love on Valentine's Day?

"Let's stick together."

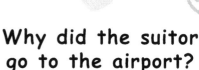

Why did the suitor go to the airport?

He wanted to buy his sweetheart plane chocolate.

Why did the geologis and the tennis refere not get along?

They kept pointing out faults.

Should we be afraid of Cupid's arrows?

He's got enough to make one quiver.

What did the florist say to his Valentine?

"Put your tulips on mine."

What do you need for the perfect Valentine candlelight dinner?

A great match.

What did the geologist say to his Valentine?

"You rock my world."

What did the male bee say to his queen bee on Valentine's Day?

"Bee-ing with you is fun."

What did the circle say to the triangle?

"You're acute one."

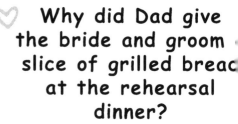

What did the Cyclops say to his date?

"Eye love you."

What did the mints say to the sad wedding cake?

"Is something eating at you?"

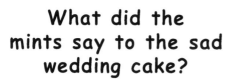

Why did Dad give the bride and groom slice of grilled bread at the rehearsal dinner?

He wanted to give them a toast.

Why couldn't the dry cleaner take time to talk to his girlfriend when she came by the store to visit?

He had pressing business.

How emotional are most weddings?

Very, even the cake is often in tiers.

Why did the girl give up on her romance with the Chinese chef?

She saw him wokking away.

Why were vegetables hired to be musicians at the Valentine's Day Dance?

People love dancing to the beet.

Why did the shy female snake feel uncomfortable around the boa constrictor?

She felt he had a crush on her.

How did the weightlifter know he was in love?

He had strong feelings.

Why did the jumper cable fall in love with the car battery?

When he first met her, there was a spark between them.

Why did the fiddle-playing musician break up with his girlfriend?

She refused to play second fiddle.

Why was the river rafter so agreeable to whatever his girlfriend wanted?

He always went with the flow.

14

Why did the two magnets fall in love?

They were very attracted to each other.

Cupid is known for bow hunting; what happened when Dad went bow hunting?

He found five bows, ten pieces of uncurled ribbon, tissue paper, and two gift bags.

How long did the candlelight romance last?

A wick.

54

Why did the baker's girlfriend break up with him?

He was too kneady.

Why did the carpenter not give his girlfriend flowers for Valentine's Day?

The floorist didn't have any.

What did the pianist say to the organist on Valentine's Day?

"I like how we get along so well; we are always in a chord."

Why did the girl bring duct tape to the gym when she went on a blind date?

She heard some of the body builders were ripped.

What do you call the type of love that results when an engagement is called off?

It is love to no a veil.

Why did the groom seek quality people for the wedding ceremony?

His wife-to-be asked him to find the Best Man.

What kind of wedding did the two cellphone have?

It was a double-ring ceremony.

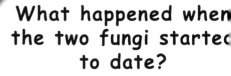

What happened when the two fungi started to date?

They took a lichen to each other.

Why did the plumber break up with his girlfriend?

Because their relationship went down the drain.

Why did the raisin go to the dance with the peanut?

He couldn't find a date.

What did the boy bat say to the girl bat on Valentine's Day?

"Do you want to hang around together?"

What did one tooth ask the other tooth on Valentine's Day?

"Is the dentist taking you out tonight?"

Why did the girl think the optometrist was in love with her even though he wasn't?

Because as he handed her a package of glass-cleaning wipes, he said, "Eye care for you."

What did the woman say about her husband who shredded cheese for a living?

"He's a grate guy."

How did the two geologists do on their Valentine's date together?

They were on the rocks.

Why should you send flowers every Valentine's Day and not just this year?

Because flowers are not meant to be once and floral (for all).

What happened when the boy gave hi girlfriend an icecrean cone consisting of chocolate, nuts, and marshmallow instead of just chocolate?

It was a rocky road.

What did the historia say to his sweetheart

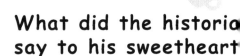

"I know a lot about important dates. Wan to go on one with me?"

Why did the hero give his girlfriend a flower?

Because he rose to the occasion.

What did the skeleton miss most about his former girlfriend?

Her spine; he told everyone he really wanted her back.

What did the sailor say to his jealous girlfriend on Valentine's Day?

"I only have ayes for you."

Why was the boy bored watching his girlfriend's favorite soap with her?

For three straight hours, all they did was sit on the bathroom floor and stared at the soap dish.

What did one student say to the other student as they walked hand-in-hand toward the gym?

"Do you think we will work out?"

Why did the girl maple tree fall in love with the boy maple tree?

He was sappy.

What letter did the priest admit giving a mispronunciation?

He said, "I pronounce 'U' 'man and wife'."

Why did the boy give the girl a six-week-old dog for Valentine's Day?

They had puppy love.

What compliment did the postal carrier receive both for delivering all the Valentine's Day mail and for his job of being a comedian at the comedy club?

"You have great delivery skills."

What did the peanut say to the almond?

"People will think we are nuts, but let's get married anyway."

Why did the burger not take his new girlfriend Patty to the barbeque?

He worried an old flame might be there.

Why does Cupid's arrow often miss his target and hit someone else?

Cupid's bow has a drawback.

What did Venus say
to the sun?

"You're so hot."

What kind of date
did the two musicians
have?

Noteworthy.

Why was the U.S.
girl so frustrated with
the lottery ticket her
boyfriend gave her for
Valentine's Day?

It didn't make any
cents to her.

As the teenage
sweethearts swung
on the swing set at
the park, what kind
of conversation did
they have?

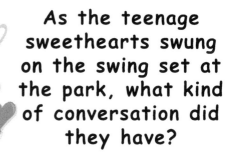

A back and forth one

What change did the
English teacher tell
his girlfriend that he
wanted to make to
the alphabet?

"Let's put U and I
together."

What type of joke
should you tell about
that notch in the bac
of Cupid's arrow?

A notch-notch joke.

How easy did Dad think that feeding his daughter's wedding guests at the reception would be?

A piece of cake.

Card Three
Silly Scenarios and Wise Saying

"You always gain by giving love."
~ **Reese Witherspoon**

Love seldom goes as expected. Due to miscommunication and freak accidents, the most well intentioned love can go awry. Blame it on Cupid for not shooting an arrow correctly or on fate itself, but love is a roller-coaster of emotions. No matter how big the stress, though, love can conquer all.

Although they are not funny as one goes through them, these ups-and-downs are extremely funny as one reflects upon them and they often become part of the shared experience that the relationship later builds upon. Next time you are undergoing an unexpected event, review these silly scenarios and words of wisdom and remember that other people have also had love take unexpected turns.

The groom looked nervously at the
preacher and then said to the bride,
"A, E, I, O, U, and sometimes Y."
The preacher looked at the bride and asked,
**"And do you have any vowels you wish
to say to him?"**

A young woman goes to a fortune teller to seek help with a romantic crisis – she has two men who want to become her husband – Tom and Mark, and she can't decide which to choose. She explained the situation to the fortune teller, and then the fortune teller peered into the crystal ball. As the girl watched the crystal ball and the medium's face, she suddenly noticed a change in the medium's expression and so she asked excitedly, "Tell me, who is the lucky one?"
"Tom is the lucky one."
"So, I'm going to marry Tom?" the girl sighed in relief.
"No, you're going to marry Mark. Didn't you just hear me, I said Tom was the lucky one."

Courtship is full of ups and downs. For instance, consider the highs and lows experienced by the boy in this ditty:
The nervous teenage boy walked up to the pretty girl and asked,
"May I get your number?"
The girl replied, "Do you have a pen?"
The boy was prepared.
He took a pen and paper from his pocket and said, "I do."
"Then you better get back in it before the farmer notices you are missing."

My friend had a plan to find love – he would go from one web page to another web page until he found the right girl. **He only went to one page, though – it was love at first site!**

Two middle-aged women were discussing their Valentine's Day adventures. When the first had finished sharing about her epic date, she asked her friend, "So, how was your date?" "It started off great. He pulled up in a purple 1957 Studebaker Golden Hawk. The car was immaculate, and it took my breath away." "So, what went wrong?" **"My date was the original owner."**

Many people have thoughts of love, but only a few people are gifted at putting those thoughts onto paper; therefore, on Valentine's Day many people resort to sending cards with verses by professional poets. One day, a boy came into the pharmacy looking for the perfect card. He spent literally hours reading over the cards, looking for just the right one. At last, he proclaimed, "I have found the card that expresses my sentiments exactly." "I too believe the card should be as unique as the individual," the salesclerk proclaimed as she rang up his purchase. **"Do you have more of these cards?" he asked. "I've got nine other people to send cards to as well, and this one is perfect."**

The day before Valentine's Day a nervous man walked into the flower shop, approached the green-aproned clerk who stood behind the cash register, and said, "I'd like to buy some flowers for my girlfriend."
"Certainly, sir," the salesclerk stated enthusiastically.
"What are you wanting?"
"A kiss."

Another man went to the flower shop
to get his girlfriend flowers. He too
had no idea of what she would like,
so he said to the clerk,
"I'd like some flowers."
"Orchids?" the clerk suggested.
"No kids. Just flowers."

Hearts are wild creatures, that's why our ribs are cages.

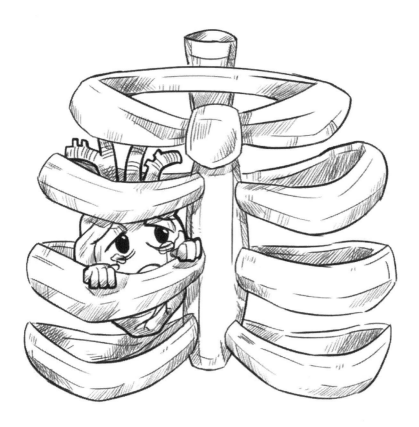

Card Four
Knock-Knock Jokes

"If you see someone without a smile, give them one of yours." ~ **Dolly Parton**

Valentine's Day is a chance for getting better acquainted. Whether it be a parent, a sibling, or a friend, take time to try to learn more about them. Knock-knock jokes remind us that relationships are always blooming. In a knock-knock joke, the receiver of the knock acknowledges the knock. The knocker then identifies themselves, but the receiver is not satisfied; the receiver wants to know more. Similarly, you should never be satisfied that you fully know someone. Keep enjoying learning about them and their adventures. One thing you can learn about your family and friends is whether they like knock-knock jokes. Share a few of the following with them and see what they think. Even the biggest grouch will likely crack a smile.

KNOCK, KNOCK.

Who's there?

Eye.

Eye who?

Eye would like to be your Valentine.

KNOCK, KNOCK.

Who's there?

Handsome.

Handsome who?

Handsome chocolate over to me please.

KNOCK, KNOCK.
Who's there?
Floral.
Floral who?
Floral the right reasons, let's keep telling jokes.

KNOCK, KNOCK.
Who's there?
Rhino.
Rhino who?
Rhino lots of Valentine knock-knock jokes.

KNOCK, KNOCK.
Who's there?
Heart.
Heart who?
Heart you had a Valentine; heard it might be me.

KNOCK, KNOCK.

Who's there?

Val N. Tines.

Val N. Tines who?

Val N. Tines Day is on February 14 again this year.

KNOCK, KNOCK.

Who's there?

Cantaloupe.

Cantaloupe who?

Cantaloupe, so we will just have to get married the traditional way.

KNOCK, KNOCK.

Who's there?

Daisy.

Daisy who?

Daisy us, and they start gossiping.

KNOCK, KNOCK.

Who's there?

Yourself.

Yourself who?

Yourself phone just received a text.

KNOCK, KNOCK.

Who's there?

Atlas.

Atlas who?

Atlas we get to celebrate Valentine's Day.

KNOCK, KNOCK.
Who's there?
Romeo.
Romeo who?
Romeo-ver to the other side of the lake, please.

KNOCK, KNOCK.
Who's there?
I. Yam.
I. Yam who?
I. Yam enjoying sharing knock-knock jokes with you.

KNOCK, KNOCK.
Who's there?
Shirley.
Shirley who?
Shirley we can come up with more knock-knock jokes.

KNOCK, KNOCK.

Who's there?

Honeydew.

Honeydew who?

Honeydew you want to be my Valentine?

KNOCK, KNOCK.
Who's there?
Roman Tick.
Roman Tick who?
Roman Tick evenings like tonight are rare, so enjoy.

KNOCK, KNOCK.
Who's there?
Fondue You.
Fondue You who?
Fondue You; I'm very, very fond of you.

KNOCK, KNOCK.
Who's there?
Rome Ants.
Rome Ants who?
Rome Ants is a way to show someone that you care.

KNOCK, KNOCK.

Who's there?

Owl.

Owl who?

Owl always love you, Valentine.

KNOCK, KNOCK.
Who's there?
Sadie.
Sadie who?
Sadie magic words and I'll be your Valentine.

KNOCK, KNOCK.
Who's there?
Thistle.
Thistle who?
Thistle be a lot of fun; I love telling Valentine knockknock jokes.

KNOCK, KNOCK.
Who's there?
Sir Tain Lee.
Sir Tain Lee who?
Sir Tain Lee is fun being here with you telling knock knock jokes.

KNOCK, KNOCK.

Who's there?

Yvonne.

Yvonne who?

Yvonne to be my Valentine?

KNOCK, KNOCK.
Who's there?
Honeybee.
Honeybee who?
Honeybee a sweetheart and be my Valentine.

KNOCK, KNOCK.

Who's there?

Stacey.

Stacey who?

Stay; see what other knock-knock jokes we can tell.

KNOCK, KNOCK.
Who's there?

Wood.

Wood who?

Wood you be my Valentine?

KNOCK, KNOCK.

Who's there?

Shore.

Shore who?

Shore would like to be your Valentine.

KNOCK, KNOCK.

Who's there?

Sid.

Sid who?

Sid down next to me, and let's tell more Valentine knockknock jokes.

Did you enjoy the book? 14

If you did, we are ecstatic. If not, please write your complaint to us, and we will ensure to fix it.

If you're feeling generous, there is something important that you can help me with – tell other people that you enjoyed the book.

Ask a grown-up to write about it on Amazon. When they do, more people will find out about the book. It also lets Amazon know that we are making kids around the world laugh. Even a few words and ratings would go a long way.

If you have any ideas or jokes that you think are super funny, please let us know. We would love to hear from you. Our email address is - **riddleland@riddlelandforkids.com**

Riddleland Bonus Book

http://pixelfy.me/riddlelandbonus

Thank you for buying this book. We would like to share a special bonus as a token of appreciation. It is a collection of 50 original jokes, riddles, and two super funny stories!

Join our **Facebook Group**
at **Riddleland for Kids** to get
daily jokes and riddles.

Would you like your jokes and riddles to be featured in our next book?

We are having a contest to see who are the smartest or funniest boys and girls in the world! :
   1) Creative and Challenging Riddles
   2) Tickle Your Funny Bone Contest

Parents, please email us your child's "Original" Riddle or Joke and **he or she could win a $25 Amazon gift card and be featured in our next book.**

Here are the rules:
   1) We're looking for super challenging riddles and extra funny jokes.
   2) Jokes and riddles MUST be 100% original—NOT something discovered on the Internet.
   3) You can submit both a joke and a riddle because they are two separate contests.
   4) Don't get help from your parents—unless they're as funny as you are.
   5) Winners will be announced via email or our Facebook group – Riddleland for Kids
   6) In your entry, please confirm which book you purchased.
   7) Email us at Riddleland@riddlelandforkids.com

Other Fun Children Books for Kids!

Riddles Series

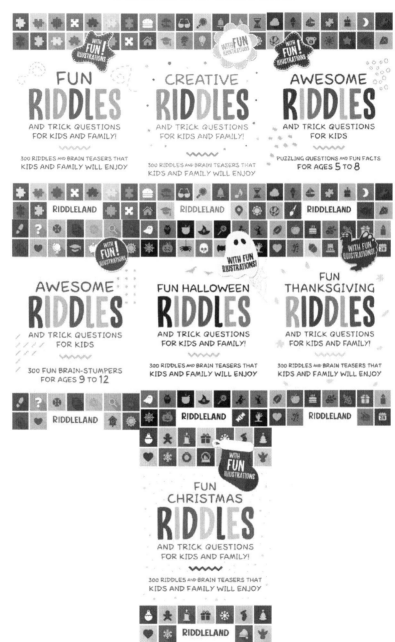

FUN
RIDDLES
AND TRICK QUESTIONS
FOR KIDS AND FAMILY!

300 RIDDLES AND BRAIN TEASERS THAT
KIDS AND FAMILY WILL ENJOY

CREATIVE
RIDDLES
AND TRICK QUESTIONS
FOR KIDS AND FAMILY!

300 RIDDLES AND BRAIN TEASERS THAT
KIDS AND FAMILY WILL ENJOY

AWESOME
RIDDLES
AND TRICK QUESTIONS
FOR KIDS

PUZZLING QUESTIONS AND FUN FACTS
FOR AGES 5 TO 8

AWESOME
RIDDLES
AND TRICK QUESTIONS
FOR KIDS

300 FUN BRAIN-STUMPERS
FOR AGES 9 TO 12

FUN HALLOWEEN
RIDDLES
AND TRICK QUESTIONS
FOR KIDS AND FAMILY!

300 RIDDLES AND BRAIN TEASERS THAT
KIDS AND FAMILY WILL ENJOY

FUN THANKSGIVING
RIDDLES
AND TRICK QUESTIONS
FOR KIDS AND FAMILY!

300 RIDDLES AND BRAIN TEASERS THAT
KIDS AND FAMILY WILL ENJOY

FUN CHRISTMAS
RIDDLES
AND TRICK QUESTIONS
FOR KIDS AND FAMILY!

300 RIDDLES AND BRAIN TEASERS THAT
KIDS AND FAMILY WILL ENJOY

The Laugh Challenge Series

Would You Rather... Series

Get them on Amazon
or our website at www.riddlelandforkids.com

About Riddleland 14

Riddleland is a mom + dad run publishing company. We are passionate about creating fun and innovative books to help children develop their reading skills and fall in love with reading. If you have suggestions for us or want to work with us, shoot us an email at riddleland@riddlelandforkids.com

Our family's favorite quote:

"Creativity is an area in which younger people have a tremendous advantage since they have an endearing habit of always questioning past wisdom and authority."
~ Bill Hewlett

Made in the USA
Middletown, DE
04 February 2021